Marx

FOR BEGINNERS

Arnd Schneider and Oscar Zarate

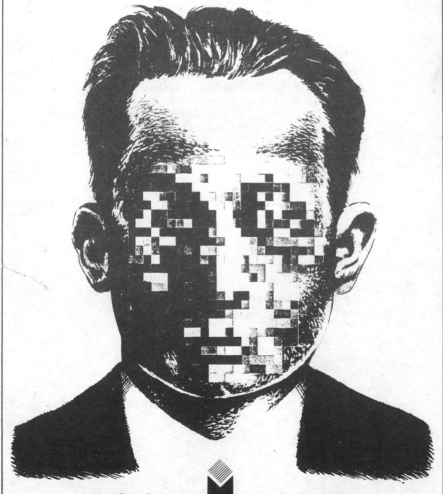

 ICON BOOKS

Published in 1994 by Icon Books Ltd.,
52 High Street, Trumpington, Cambridge CB2 2LS

Distributed in the UK, Europe and Asia by the Penguin Group:
Penguin Books Ltd, 27 Wrights Lane, London W8 5TZ

Published in Australia in 1995 by Allen & Unwin Pty. Ltd.,
PO Box 8500, 9 Atchison Street, St. Leonards, NSW 2065

Text copyright © 1994 Arnd Schneider
Illustrations copyright © 1994 Oscar Zarate

The author and artist have their moral rights.

Originating editor: Richard Appignanesi

A CIP catalogue record for this book is available from the British Library

ISBN 1 874166 20 X

Printed and bound in Great Britain by
The Bath Press, Avon

CRIME INCORPORATED

Say "organized crime", and everyone thinks "Mafia". And they also think **American** Mafia – the "godfather" at the head of a soap opera Big Business family.

Because the USA is the biggest financial empire in the world, most people imagine that the US Mafia must therefore be the biggest, richest Crime Syndicate. Not true – it is smaller than the original Sicilian Mafia.

Let's look at the Sicilian origins of the Mafia and its international expansion.

3

Why did organized Big Business crime flourish in Italy, which now ranks ahead of Britain as the world's seventh largest economy?

The first thing to get straight. Not everything is "Mafia", not even in Italy which knows other forms of criminal organizations.

And there are lots of other groups worldwide.

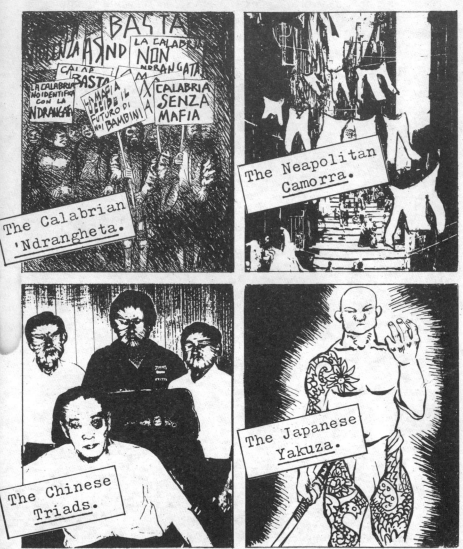

The Calabrian 'Ndrangheta.

The Neapolitan Camorra.

The Chinese Triads.

The Japanese Yakuza.

The real Mafia has its roots in Sicily where it made its huge profits and has its main recruitment base.

WHAT DOES MAFIA MEAN?

Nobody knows what the word "Mafia" means and when it originated.

In the great Mafia trials, the accused usually deny (for obvious reasons) not only their own membership in, but the very existence of, the Mafia.

Many etymologies of the word Mafia have been suggested, few are convincing.

The first mafiosi were said to be medieval Sicilian knights fighting the French in the revolt of 1282 known as the "Sicilian Vespers".

Mafia is the acronym of the rebels' battle cry:

Morte **A**i **F**rancesi **I**tália **A**nela

(Death to the French, Italy gasps!).

It would suit the Mafia, which has often perverted the Sicilian separatist cause for its own benefit, to have its origins linked to a glorious event of early Sicilian history.

The Mafia name has even been linked to the revolutionary nationalist, Giuseppe Mazzini (1805-72).

M A F I A

Mazzini **A**utorizza **F**urti **I**ncendi **A**vvelenamenti

(Mazzini authorizes thefts, arson and poisonings!)

Myths like these have encouraged an idea of the Mafia as an organization in league with Masonic and revolutionary secret societies.

Mafia crime was first specified in Palermo court proceedings of 1865 against illegal receivers (**manutengoli**).

From 1875, the term Mafia comes into international usage.

SICILY – "COLONY OF OTHERS" AT THE CENTRE OF THE MEDITERRANEAN

To understand the Mafia, we have to look at the history of Sicily where it developed. Sicily has endured an endless succession of invasions and occupations.

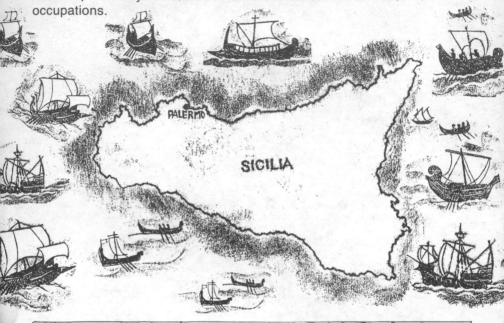

First, the Greek settlements in the mid-8th century BC . . .

And the list goes on ...

Carthaginians, Romans, Byzantines, Arabs, Normans, German Staufer, Aragonese, Catalans, Spaniards ... and finally Piedmontese and other mainland Italians.

Each of these settlers, invaders and conquerors contributed to the island's rich cultural history.

SICILY WAS NEARLY ALWAYS A DEPENDENT COLONY.

And these foreign powers levied heavy taxes and exploited Sicily's natural produce – wheat, silk, cotton, sugar cane and sulphur.

9

This series of exploitative administrations helped to create a general mistrust of all outsiders and strangers among Sicilians.

But these rebellions were sporadic and targeted at local causes (such as the Palermo hunger revolt of 1647). Contrary to common belief, such protests did not have any elaborate separatist or nationalist ideology behind them.

MISERIA ("THE MISERY")

OUR **MISERIA** IS THE FAULT OF CENTURIES OF BAD ADMINISTRATION BY **OUTSIDERS.**

THE MAFIA BEGAN AS SELF-DEFENCE GROUPS IN THESE EARLY TIMES.

AVERAGE SICILIAN (CIRCA...)

SHEFFIELD STEEL

BYZANTINE HAT

CARTHAGINIAN SHIRT

CATALAN BELT

ARAGONESE ESPADRILLE

ROMAN BOOT

This is a myth often heard – not only from separatists but from people claiming an original "Robin Hood" status for the Mafia when Sicily was unfree.

But the fact is, the opposition "native Sicilians" v/s "foreigners" doesn't make sense in the historical long term. Sicilians have always been a mix of peoples that **included** past invaders. So it doesn't help to presume an **unchanging** Sicilian identity or interests.

11

THE LATIFUNDIA SYSTEM

Since Roman times, western Sicily produced wheat on large estates (**latifondi**). In antiquity, slaves worked the land. Later on, landless labourers and sharecroppers worked for feudal landlords.

Sicily kept this role of "bread basket" almost throughout its history.

THE GABELLOTTI

After the abolition of feudalism in 1812, the administrators (the **gabellotti**) of large, formerly baronial estates began to buy, rent or illegally occupy vast areas of Church and common lands, which enlarged both the size and number of the great estates.

THE NUMBER OF LANDLESS WORKERS, SMALL TENANTS AND SHARECROPPERS INCREASED...

WHILE THE NUMBER OF PROPRIETOR PEASANTS DECLINED.

AND WE **GABELLOTTI** BECAME THE LOCALLY DOMINANT POWER BROKERS!

Gabellotti rented the large estates from absentee noble landlords.

THE MEZZADRIA SYSTEM

The **gabellotti** then sublet the estates in tiny plots of 2 to 4 hectares to their sharecroppers. This sharecropping system is known in Southern Italy as **mezzadria**, meaning "half tenancy", in fact one of the most unjust tenancy arrangements.

I PROVIDE YOU WITH THE SEEDS AND YOU OWE ME $\frac{2}{3}$ OR $\frac{3}{4}$ OF THE HARVEST —

PLUS, ALSO MAINTAIN THE BUILDINGS, PROVIDE THE **CAMPIERI** (GUARDS) WITH FOOD —

AND DELIVER BREAD, WINE AND VEGETABLES TO THE **GABELLOTTO!**

MEDIEVAL FEUDAL TITHES SEEM MILD IN COMPARISON!

Such "debt-peonage" (from **peones**, landless workers on Latin American great estates) is typical of rent capitalism in both Southern Europe and Latin America.

15

In Sicily, rent capitalism allowed the gabellotti to control the lives of an entire segment of the rural population.

They also fulfilled functions as arbitrators within the villages and the outside world.

These gabellotti were the first mafiosi.

THE UNIFICATION OF ITALY

Italy was a disunified patchwork of small states until 1860. The northern kingdom of Piedmont, in the reign of Victor Emmanuel II (1820-78), was the dominant unifying force. Sicily had unsuccessfully rebelled in 1848 against the Bourbon king ruling from Naples.

On 11 May 1860, the freelance revolutionary Giuseppe Garibaldi (1807-82) landed in Marsala, Sicily, with his famous band the **Mille** (the One Thousand). He fought a brilliant guerrilla war against a vastly superior Bourbon army, which he quickly defeated, and proclaimed himself dictator ruling on behalf of King Victor Emmanuel. His charisma won him the support of the bewildered Sicilians, who began to venerate him as a saint.

In Otober 1860, Garibaldi declared a plesbiscite which resulted in a 99.5% vote for unification with Italy under the Piedmontese king, rather than opting for autonomy. Sicilians soon grew to hate their new Piedmontese master who treated them like a colony. Moreover, while Northern Italy began to benefit from industrial development, Sicily and the South sank into economic and social stagnation which favoured the Mafia.

17

Let's look at the world of mafiosi in a small town near Corleone in Western Sicily in 1860, the year of Italy's unification.

Franco, son of a small tenant farmer, is part of a bandit gang engaged in infringement of pasture rights, animal theft and blackmailing.

THE BENVENUTO FAMILY

The Benevenutos were a family of gabellotti.

FIRST, A WARNING...

The Benvenutos warn Franco's family whom they perceive as rivals.

One of Benvenutos' field guards (**campiere**) meets Franco's father on a footpath.

THE NEXT WARNING...

A sign – they could have used others, like breaking the legs of donkeys or mules, or cutting the throat of a sheep.

But the Mafia only kills as a last resort. Most accounts of their murders are stories of "deaths foretold", with their victims already knowing their fate.

FINALLY, THE KILLING...

When the Benvenutos' killers couldn't find Franco himself...

It seemed natural to local people that Franco would come back one day to revenge himself on old Salvatore Benvenuto who had ordered the killings.

VENDETTA

Franco returned in 1871. He let loose some cattle on Salvatore Benvenuto's fields. Salvatore, then in his seventies, went with a friend to inspect the damage.

From the bank of a small path, Franco jumped on the back of Salvatore's mule.

While they were riding, Franco slowly butchered old Salvatore.

Franco fled, but was caught years later and given a life sentence.

Franco might be a cattle thief, infringer of pasture rights and occasional extortionist of the rich – but was not a mafioso.

His own criminal activities simply challenged the power of the new **padroni** (masters) of the area.

The abolition of feudalism in 1812 and the dissolution of Church lands in 1860 were reforms meant to benefit smallholders, peasants and day labourers.

AH **MISERIA!** THE OLD FEUDAL LANDLORDS WERE REPLACED BY EVEN MORE RUTHLESS GABELLOTTI!

What was intended as a land reform simply benefited a new class of rural entrepreneurs. In their voracious appetite for more land, the gabellotti grabbed the common lands, where, at least under feudalism, peasants enjoyed the usufruct rights of pasture, cutting wood and hunting.

When common lands are no longer available to local people, it seems understandable that small tenant folk like Franco would turn to "other" forms of income.

These **banditi** would suddenly attack the new rich and distribute some of the loot to the poor – or, at least, that's what the village people said. But they also attacked the occasional traveller and salesman.

The Benvenutos finally got their come-uppance in 1914 from the Castelli gang, notoriously violent bandits used by the rising Turoni and Rubino Mafia clans.

COSCHE –
THE ARTICHOKE PRINCIPLE

We've seen a typical story from a place near Corleone which itself gained notoriety through the film of Mario Puzo's novel, **The Godfather**.

BUT HOW DOES THE MAFIA REALLY WORK?

LIKE THIS – SEE?

AN ARTICHOKE.

The trunk of the artichoke (**cosca**, plural **cosche**) symbolizes the mafioso and its leaves his clients – a downward structure of command based on clientelism and kinship ties. Mafia "organization" is no more complicated than this – a system of exchanging favours between strong patrons and weak clients.

"DO ME A LITTLE FAVOUR."

Between m (mafioso) and a, b, c, **favori** (favours) are exchanged.

31

The mafioso can demand favours from those he protects (such as information, votes for the mafioso's political patron, illegal actions).

The "favoured" are often already in dependent positions of kinship, friendship or employees of the mafioso's legal business.

OMERTÀ: THE CODE OF SILENCE

The client relationship will persist only so long as the exchange of favours is not interrupted. The mafioso must deliver his **promise**, after execution of his orders, and protect a, b and c.

Omertà, derivative of **uomo** (man), assumes that any dispute is a private concern between men, and does not concern the state.

CRIMES OF HONOUR

There are "crimes of honour" (**delitti d'onore**) unrelated to Mafia crime, but the fruit of a particular concept of honour. Kinship, friendship and godparenthood in Sicily carry binding moral obligations. Fathers, sons and kin must help each other unconditionally.

WE HAVE TO GUARD THE FAMILY'S HONOUR...

AND TAKE REVENGE FOR ANY SHAME DONE TO OUR WOMEN!

Rape, adultery, extramarital sex are privately punishable. If a ·man's honour is challenged, it is his duty to restore it by violence. This idea of the **moral solidarity** of the family, prevailing over all other forms of community or state, explains the long-standing **vendettas** (blood feuds).

FICTIONAL KINSHIP

Godparenthood is another traditional means of extending the network of social obligation and favours – putting **friendship** on a par with **kinship**.

But the point is, the Mafia exploits these ready-made social customs of family honour and godfatherhood for its own ends.

THE PARTITO

Our structure of the Mafia network is still incomplete. In order to operate, the mafioso needs protection from above, from **political** patrons with whom he exchanges favours for **their** protection.

Obviously, there must be no direct communication between a, b and c and the patrons. The mafioso acts as power-broker mediating between the top and bottom levels. This relationship between mafiosi and higher political patrons is called **partito**. This, plus the code of **omertà** observed by fellow mafiosi and clients, will allow the mafioso to go unpunished for his crimes.

MEN OF HONOUR

Mafiosi were originally **rural entrepreneurs** operating in the small agricultural towns of Western Sicily and respected as **galantuomini** (gentlemen) or **uomini d'onore** (men of honour).

This is how Genco Russo of Mussomeli – after World War II, second only to Don Calò of Villalba (Calogera Vizzini) – saw himself.

I WAS BORN THIS WAY. ACTING WITHOUT ULTERIOR MOTIVES. IT DOESN'T MATTER WHO YOU ARE, ASK ME A FAVOUR, I DO IT. THAT'S MY NATURE.

HUMAN NATURE.

WE'RE MADE THAT WAY. IT'S FELLOW FEELING. YOU COULD SAY IT'S MY WHOLE TEMPERAMENT, MY CHARACTER. PEOPLE CAN IDENTIFY WITH ME. WHY IS IT THEY ALL FLOCK TO ME?

A MAN'LL COME TO ME: "I HAVE A BONE TO PICK WITH X COULD YOU HELP ME OUT?"

I GET AHOLD OF X, HERE OR AT HIS PLACE, IT'S ALL A MATTER OF DIPLOMACY. WE MAKE PEACE. LOOK, I'M NOT TRYING TO TOOT MY OWN HORN, LET'S BE PERFECTLY CLEAR. YOU'VE COME ALL THIS WAY TO SEE ME, SO I'M JUST BEING HOSPITABLE.

I'VE NEVER BEEN GUILTY OF VANITY OR AMBITION.

I HAVE OPEN ARMS FOR EVERY SIZE AND SHAPE.

WHAT ABOUT POLITICS? ONLY IF I CAN DO GOOD. THERE'S NOTHING IN IT FOR ME. I DON'T HAVE MY FINGER IN ANYBODY'S PIE.

DO I RESPECT PRIESTS? ABSOLUTELY. I RESPECT RELIGION. I MEAN THE HOLY ROMAN CATHOLIC KIND. WHAT YOU ARE I RESPECT.

TOMORROW, FOR EXAMPLE, I HAVE TO LEAVE MY FLAIL, MY ANIMALS, EVERYTHING TO TRAVEL TO AGRIGENTO AND SAY A GOOD WORD FOR SOMEBODY, SO THAT HE WILL PASS HIS EXAMS.

In the 1960s, Genco Russo's attitude would have been shared by most people in rural Western Sicily.

DON GENCO ARBITRATES IN OUR LOCAL DISPUTES.

HE RECOMMENDS PEOPLE AND GRANTS FAVOURS.

HE HAS THE RIGHT CONNECTIONS WITH THE POLITICIANS IN PALERMO!

THE PRIVATIZATION OF SOCIAL JUSTICE

Russo and his clients make it clear. Mafia is less an organization than an **idea**. It is not a "secret society" or a single large-scale criminal association, but a way of life – an **attitude of mind**.

We can now see what is "in place" for the Mafia to operate.

1. Real kinship relationships, combined with extended (fictional) kinship – that is, both legitimate and mafia godparenthood – protect **local autonomy of action** against interference from the central state and its agents (i.e., the police).

2. The loose **cosche** structure of the Mafia clans, with their "favours programme" based on clientelism, protected by political patronage (the **partito**), characterize the effective social operation of mafia groups.

3. Violence was not only a legitimate defence of the nuclear family. Rural bandits or brigands (sometimes called "social bandits") channelled latent demands for social justice in an unjust society through a violent kind of "re-distribution of wealth". Bandits kept up a constant level of violence in the countryside. They must not, however, be confused with mafiosi, even though some later Mafia specialities, such as blackmail letters and kidnapping now practised as a veritable industry by the Calabrian **'Ndrangheta**, were first invented by bandits.

THE LUPARA

The violently enforced code of **omertà** (silence) has until very recently frustrated the attempts by police and courts to bring the Mafia to justice.

Lupara bianca (white lupara) refers to making victims disappear without trace – for instance, cementing them in a new building.

INSUFFICIENT EVIDENCE

Endless stories of revenge killings are a constant "healthy reminder".

Trials are abandoned because of chronic "insufficient evidence".

A woman near Palermo gained local fame because she died of natural causes in old age.

MY HEALTH HAD HAD BEEN GRAVELY ENDANGERED BY TESTIFYING AT A MAFIA TRIAL.

Those who break **omertà** – like modern supergrass Tommaso Buscetta – have to live in high security prisons or in constant hiding.

SPECIFIC CONDITIONS FOR MAFIA DEVELOPMENT

A question remains. Why did the Mafia first take root in a specific region – Western Sicily – and not in others? To answer this, let's step outside Sicily and look at another region, the Plain of Gioia Tauro in Calabria, a province of Southern Italy. This is a region of middle-sized agriculture – olive oil, wine and citrus fruits are the specialities here.

In other words, a "mafia" cannot grow where there is either **small individual landowning** or **latifundist huge estates** which have no **gabellotti**-style middle men as in Sicily.

GIOIA TAURO ALLOWS US ROOM TO EXPAND – TO EXPORT TO NATIONAL AND INTERNATIONAL MARKETS.

BIG PROFITS HERE FOR THE SMART INVESTOR.

BUT BIG LOSSES TOO IF PRICES FALL!

Gioia Tauro attracted "venture capitalists" to its profitable medium-scale agriculture and food-processing industry. But specialized agriculture is vulnerable to price fluctuations on the open market.

The entrepreneurs who took control in Gioia Tauro were the first Calabrian "mafiosi".

They adopted the familiar codes of honour and violence to regulate market forces and monopolize the transfer of resources from the local level to the urban centres.

ITALY AFTER UNIFICATION

Western Sicily already had the perfect Mafia scenario – vast latifundia estates with gabellotti, dependent sharecroppers and landless wage labourers.

The welding together of Italy into a unified state was additional good news to the Mafia – because it extended both its **market** and **political patronage**.

A UNIFIED ITALY AFTER 1860 MEANS A BIGGER MARKET!

WE CAN EXPORT MORE WHEAT WITHOUT TARIFFS.

51

THE CATTLE TRAIL TO AN URBAN MAFIA

Rural Mafia clans in the second half of the 19th century specialized in livestock thefts, especially in the Western provinces of Palermo, Trapani, Girgenti (now Agrigento) and Caltanisetta.

THE "U PIZZU" SCAM

But who are these "mafiosi" cattle thieves? In fact, gabellotti, field guards and cattle traders who profit **twice** from the cattle thefts.

U pizzu – or protection payments against cattle theft and damage to crops, originally demanded in "naturals" (grain) – were extorted from peasants, sharecroppers and even landowners when the mafiosi felt strong enough. By the early 20th century, the Mafia **cosche** had divided Western Sicily into territories of **u pizzu** as a tributary system.

Cattle-rustling first linked the interior with the coastal cities – the capital Palermo foremost – and opened up new urban routes of communication.

By the end of the 19th century, rural mafiosi had absorbed urban petty crime and introduced a crucial new racket...

Mafiosi gained monopoly positions in local industry and trade as wholesalers and entrepreneurs.

55

THE GOLDEN SHELL

Mafia clans were particularly attracted to the **Conca d'Oro** – the Golden Shell – an area of intensive farming on the bay of Palermo, famous for its endless orange and lemon orchards and vegetable gardens.

Mafia entrepreneurs "protected" this area and controlled water distribution to landowners and small tenants.

As wholesalers, they also dictated the market price of fruit and vegetables.

A similar control was established over the city's cattle markets, abattoirs and food-processing plants.

THE MAFIA AND FASCISM

In 1922, Benito Mussolini came to power as Italy's dictator, and a Fascist totalitarian regime was installed for the next 21 years.

The new Fascist masters could not tolerate the Mafia's stranglehold monopoly in Sicily and the stretch of its tentacles into Italian society.

In 1926 and 1927, Cesare Mori, the Fascist Prefect of Palermo, carried out mass raids on the Mafia. Mori used every kind of inquisitional method, including torture and the arrest without trial of thousands of innocent people.

Many mafiosi were also jailed or exiled to remote islands or the North of Italy (where, ironically, they were particularly well placed to expand the Mafia's interests after World War Two).

Despite the publicity that Mori's draconian measures attracted,
he never succeeded to "finish off" the Mafia, as was popularly believed.
The Mafia's classical "broker" functions, such as the manipulation
of local elections, were suspended.

Many mafiosi still had powerful enough contacts with their **partito** (the protecting politicians) to avoid arrest.

Other mafiosi went to Tunis or emigrated to the US and reinforced the American Cosa Nostra.

Others again went into "inner emigration", disguising themselves as local Fascist dignitaries – only to reappear in their true colours after the downfall of the Fascist regime in 1943.

THE MAFIA IN AMERICA: 1ST PHASE JOE PETROSINO'S STORY

The transcontinental links between the Sicilian Mafia and America's early Cosa Nostra first aroused the suspicion of the US authorities at the beginning of the century.

In 1908, Joseph Petrosino of the Italian department of the New York police got permission from his boss Theodor Bingham to travel to Sicily. There he would investigate the relationship between the Sicilian Mafia and the so-called Black Hand (**Mano Nera**), as the Cosa Nostra was then called.

I WANT TO ESTABLISH CONTACTS WITH THE ITALIAN POLICE AND PREVENT THE IMMIGRATION OF CRIMINALS.

Petrosino, of Italian extraction, had already repatriated 600 Italian criminals who specialized in extortion rackets in America's immigrant "Little Italy" ghettos.

With 30 years experience of service, he knew what was at stake and arranged his journey with utmost secrecy, travelling under the name of Guglielmo De Simone, with an address at the Banca Commerciale of Palermo.

Unfortunately, the press leaked details of Petrosino's mission, and the Black Hand bosses were alerted. These chieftains hastily convened a meeting in New Orleans, home to the oldest Sicilian immigrant community in the US.

Don Vito had been pivotal in modernizing the Sicilian Mafia, integrating hinterland and coastal areas, making big business out of extortion and kidnappings, and also organizing the emigration of mafiosi to the United States.

Petrosino arrived in Italy on 20 February 1909 and was received by Minister of the Interior Peano.

On a Saturday night 12 March 1909, as Petrosino crossed Palermo's Marina Square, a man fired three shots from a revolver. Petrosino managed to return fire, but did not hit his assassin who had mortally wounded him in the head.

Legend says that the assassin was Don Vito Cascio Ferro himself who had personally accepted to liquidate the American police investigator.

Don Vito had supper with some illustrious friends, interrupted it for two hours to kill Petrosino, and returned to these people who would testify that he had stayed all evening with them.

Don Vito was never tried, and when during Fascism he landed in jail, he made a famous remark.

Such arrogant assumption of lack of any evidence against mafiosi (thanks to the code of **omertà** which discourages witnesses) has remained typical to the present.

THE BLACK HAND LETTER

In the United States, the Black Hand confined itself to the "little Italy" immigrant ghettos. It could rely on cultural codes of honour and silence, and thereby organize extortion and protection rackets.

In 1908, an Italian reform society, called rightly enough "The White Hand", published its report on the Black Hand's practice of blackmail letters.

The letter in its classic form is short, written in an unassuming and sometimes friendly tone.

I CAN'T READ IT. WHAT DOES IT SAY, MARIA?

IT REQUESTS MONEY AND SAYS WHERE TO DELIVER IT.

The request also contains a threat, sometimes veiled by mysterious allusions, sometimes expressed with brutality.

At the place designated
the victim does not find
anybody.
But a few days later a second
letter repeats the request
for money and also the
threat in aggravated form.

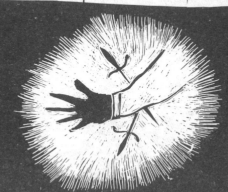

Then comes a third and fourth letter,
each with more violent threats expressed
either in words or symbols —
such as drawings of
pierced hearts,
daggers,
pistols,
crosses,

skulls and crossbones,
bombs, etc.

A SOLICITOUS FRIEND...

The victim is intimidated to such a point that he applies for the help of "friends". Some phrase in a letter will hint vaguely at so-called friends; suggesting that whoever seeks will find – that somebody might intervene between the victim and the mysterious and terrible god that made the demand.

This "solicitous friend" is to be the intermediary, but who in reality is the accomplice if not the author of the blackmail. He is indicated with sufficient precision. So the unfortunate victim finally seeks out the "friend" who can save him . . . and he has no difficulty whatever in finding him.

In the ghettos, it is considered bad form to discuss such affairs. If a man is murdered, he is spoken of as the "poor disgraced one"; murders or persecutions are simply "trouble".

Certain men are called "mafiosi", but this means only that they are domineering, swaggering, fearless, and no one would dare make a direct accusation. Black Hand is a term used only jokingly, and the words **omertà** and **vendetta** are never heard.

No one is so despised as an informer. Showing interest in others' affairs is not desirable. Men who are murdered are generally believed to have deserved their fate – and these victims are not buried from the church unless a large sum is paid for a special mass.

PROHIBITION

The development of the American Cosa Nostra was not a result of mafiosi exported from Sicily (or expelled by Fascists in the 1920s and 30s). Italian immigrant ghettos themselves provided the seedbed, but the extortion racketeers were not organized in large syndicates. Italo-American gangs remained secondary to Irish, and later, Jewish gangs in the first two decades of the century.

Things began to change in the latter half of the 1920s, during the Prohibition era (1920-33). Italian immigrants became bootleg distillers and Cosa Nostra men distributed the hootch in conjunction with more powerful Jewish gangsters.

Prohibition made it illegal to distil, sell or drink alcohol. This unique US Federal law was the outcome of lobbying by a powerful Temperance Movement, strongly supported by early feminists. It remains a lesson and a warning that the criminalization of any substance (alcohol, drugs) creates an **illegal market** that will be supplied by organized crime.

73

Also at this time – and into the 30s and 40s – Italo-American mafiosi left the ghettos and escalated into gambling, prostitution and drugs – activities traditionally despised by the Sicilian Mafia.

A new Cosa Nostra criminal culture had "matured" in a style more like American mobsters than Sicilian mafiosi – or "men of honour".

74

GANGLAND WARS

This new breed of mobsters began violently to replace the earlier ethnically organized Irish and Jewish gangsters, both within the ghettos and outside, operating in different "families" and syndicates across the US.

This period of expansion (from 1925 to the 40s) became notorious for rival ethnic gangland wars – but also for conflicts between Italo-American syndicates, for instance, the more modern Cosa Nostra against the traditional Unione Siciliana which did not care to expand into prostitution.

These territorial wars nevertheless involved some cross-ethnic alliances, which explains why influential non-Italian gangsters like Meyer Lansky and Bugsy Siegel were on the board of the Unione Siciliana, centralized after 1931 under the command of the "infamous" Lucky Luciano. Other ethnic bosses, like Dutch Schultz, were on the losing side. 75

SCARFACE
AND THE MASSACRE

Al "Scarface" Capone, imported from New York to Chicago in the early 1920s, had played bodyguard to the syndicate boss Johnny Torrio. In 1924, Torrio was made to "abdicate" in favour of Capone after almost losing his life in an ambush.

On a wintry St Valentine's Day in 1929, some of Capone's torpedoes disguised as policemen, armed with tommyguns and a shotgun, butchered six top figures of the rival Bugs Moran gang in the S.M.C. Cartage Co. garage. A seventh victim, R.H. Schwimmer, a reputable optometrist, had the misfortune of being a "gang buff" – someone who hangs out with mobsters for the kicks.

Although Scarface was holidaying in Biscayne Bay, Florida, he was blamed for the massacre.

A COSA NOSTRA PROFILE

Based on the revelations of Joe Valachi in 1965, an early Cosa Nostra supergrass, Inspector John Shanley of the New York police could report to the crime sub-commission on the essential features of the Cosa Nostra's internal structure.

No direct crime involvement of the **capi**.

According to position, age and authority, respect is demanded which is rigorously observed. The position of a person can be discerned from the tone of his voice, doors opened when he passes by, and seats offered to him.

The **capi** are in contact with their inferiors through a protective system of intermediaries. No **capo** can be approached directly from the lower ranks.

When necessary, members of a family themselves take disciplinary actions against disobedient members. Punishments can vary from simple sanctions to assassinations – and in the latter, every care is taken to leave no trace of the crime. The police will consider it a case of "disappearance". (These "disappearances" resemble the techniques of "state terrorism" employed by death squads in Latin America, and occasionally by Western secret service agencies.)

Money from illegal activities is managed (laundered) by a respected businessman – a partner of the **capo** – who invests it in imports, real estate, bonds, shares, etc. The point is always to appear respectable and correct to the public.

79

LUCKY'S WAR:
A TRANSATLANTIC ALLIANCE

On 10 July 1943, the Allies landed in Sicily – American forces in the West of the island, British in the East. The Americans advanced much faster and with less bloodshed than the British who met fierce resistance from Italian and German troops.

The answer is – according to legend – that US Naval Intelligence approached Cosa Nostra boss Lucky Luciano to fix a deal with Sicilian **capi** Mafiosi who would make the invasion a walk-in.

The fact is, Lucky's 30-year sentence was dramatically cut, and he was deported to Sicily on 9 February 1946. Why did the US authorities set Lucky free? Some say it was a reward for helping the US Navy deal with Nazi sabotage on the New York waterfront. Others deny this, asserting that Lucky while in prison could not control the New York waterfront "families". Besides, the Cosa Nostra was out of touch with wartime Sicily, and Cesare Mori's Fascist persecution had succeeded to "disconnect" the Sicilian underworld.

Let's look at the controversial legend of Lucky's "intervention". Just four days after the American landing on the Sicilian West coast, a US plane flew low over Villalba, home town of Don Calò (Calogero Vizzini), capo Mafia of the region, and dropped a parcel containing a yellow silk handkerchief monogrammed with a black L near Don Calò's doorstep.

THIS IS LUCKY LUCIANO'S SIGN.

DON GENCO IT'S TIME WE PAID OUR TROOPS A VISIT.

Don Calò and his second in command, Genco Russo, a gabellotto of the large Polizello estate near Mussomeli, then persuaded a greater part of the Italian troops supposed to defend the Western area to change their uniforms for civilian clothes, and desert, or not to fight at all.

THE POST-WAR MAFIA GROWTH

"Charlie Lucky" Luciano (born Salvatore Lucania) settled in Naples after his deportation, where he greatly furthered the Mafia's post-war growth as most powerful of all bosses, with US and Sicilian liaisons, till his death in 1962.

The Mafia was expert at providing the US Occupation authorities with everything that **AMGOT** (the provisional Allied Military Government) required.

The official interpreter at US Army HQ near Naples was Vito Genovese, Mafia racketeer, killer and Lucky's longtime underboss in New York, hiding in Italy to dodge a US murder charge.

THE COLD WAR...

The years immediately after World War II saw great political tension in Italy – a crucial time when its post-war political system would be laid down for the next 40 years.

The heroic struggles of the Italian Resistance represented a moment of hope. Partisans had fought a hard guerrilla war against both Italian Fascists and Nazi forces, culminating in the execution of Mussolini by partisans in 1945.

There was evident disunity among partisans of different stripes – Communist, liberal and nationalist tendencies.

...AND THE "NEW WORLD ORDER"

Meanwhile, the Cold War era had begun – the anti-Communist "free world" versus the Soviet bloc – a climate that would prove highly beneficial to Mafia interests.

America's geo-strategic aims favoured the rise to power of the newly founded anti-Communist Christian Democrats (DC), a Cold War policy which gave the DC licence to rule – which it did uninterruptedly till the 1990s.

THE SOUTHERN QUESTION

What means could the Christian Democrats use to ensure its one party rule in Sicily (and throughout Italy)? The situation in the South of Italy had long been desperate for urban workers, landless labourers and small sharecroppers.

NOTHING'S CHANGED – THE LAND IS STILL CONTROLLED BY LARGE ESTATES AND GABELLOTTI.

The people, inspired by post-war leftwing hopes, began to occupy the big estates and agitate for a fair distribution of the land. Estate owners, politicians and mafiosi did not stomach this.

WHAT ARE WE GOING TO DO ABOUT THESE AGITATORS?

COMMUNISTS – EVERY LAST ONE OF THEM!

SIGNORI, I HAVE AN IDEA.. LET'S CALL IN SALVATORE GIULIANO!

Alla Mattina apena alzata
o Bella ciao Bella ciao Bella ciao

Alla Mattina appena alzata
in risaia mi tocca andar

THE MASSACRE AT PORTELLA DELLA GINESTRA

Landowners and mafiosi turned to Salvatore Giuliano for help. Giuliano, twenty-three years old, was the "King of bandits". He began his career as a Robin Hood, a separatist dreaming of Sicilian independence.

E FRA GLI INSETTI E LE ZANZARE
O BELLA CIAO, BELLA CIAO, BELLA CIAO
E FRA GLI INSETTI E LE ZANZARE
UN DUR LAVORO MI TOCCA FAR

IL CAPO IN PIEDI COL SUO BASTONE
O BELLA CIAO, BELLA CIAO, BELLA CIAO,
CIAO, CIAO.

Despite intimidation by the Church, estate landlords and their mafiosi gunmen, Sicilian peasants voted against the Christian Democrats and in favour of Communist-inspired land reform on 20 April 1947.

On May Day 1947, a countryside rally gathered at Portella della Ginestra. On orders from the Mafia barons, Giuliano's band machine-gunned the crowd, killing 11 people and wounding 55.

Giuliano's massacre plans (and the source of his orders) were known to the police, Christian Democrat bosses and possibly too, the military intelligence services.

The land reform act of 1950 had no real effect, except to increase the power of gabellotti and mafiosi who reorganized themselves in large cooperatives and sublet the land under the old exploitative **mezzadria** system. (Some even wanted Sicily to become the 46th state of the US. Giuliano and mafiosi with Cosa Nostra interests supported this. To counter the separatist movement, Sicily was declared an autonomous region in 1946.)

89

POST-WAR RECONSTRUCTION AND DEVELOPMENT

Italy's economy boomed in the 1950s and 60s, and the **Cassa per il Messogiorno**, a huge development institution, distributed funds in the South. Sicily's capital, Palermo, proliferated with new bureaucracies.

The Mafia infiltrated these post-war development bureaucracies on a big scale.

Mafiosi already controlled most sectors of Palermo's urban economy, but now they extended their grip over state-administered reconstruction and development funds.

At this time, the Mafia also first began to combine "legitimate" big business (construction) with international illegal trade (drugs).

Palermo had been severely damaged by the war. A quarter of its half-million population lived in slums and 14,000 in shantytowns. Christian Democrats governed the city council for the first time in 1952 and represented the aristocratic power élite, the Church and speculators.

The new DC municipal administration fast designated large areas of the city's surroundings as "urban extension zones".

A period of frenetic building and speculation, especially in the public housing sector, occurred between 1957 and 1963.

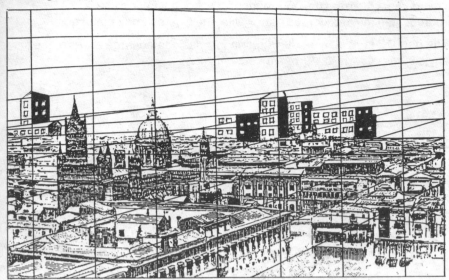

The speculators' profits from increased land values alone have been estimated at $660 million.

In a single decade, the city's appearance had been transformed – the "extension zones" dominated ever since by high-rise residential middle and upper middle class blocks and council estates.

The lack of any comprehensive city planning in this decade was the deliberate result of a deal between Vito Ciancimino, elected mayor of Palermo in 1958 after being Assessor of Public Works, and his successor at the Public Works Office, Salvo Lima (later Member of the European Parliament, assassinated by the Mafia in 1992).

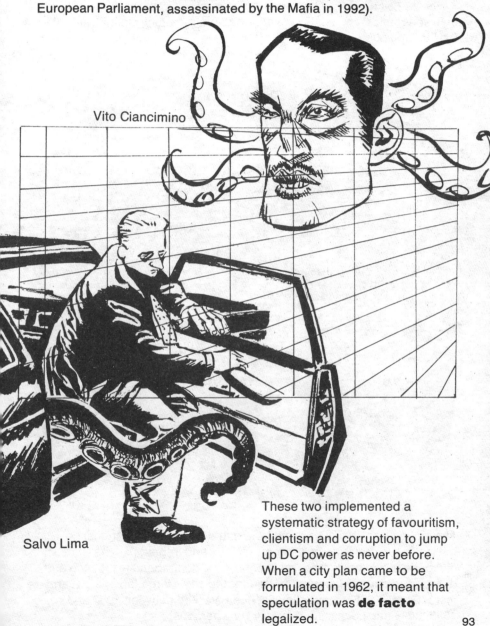

Vito Ciancimino

Salvo Lima

These two implemented a systematic strategy of favouritism, clientism and corruption to jump up DC power as never before. When a city plan came to be formulated in 1962, it meant that speculation was **de facto** legalized.

WITH POWER
COMES RESPECTABILITY

As the 1972 Anti-Mafia Commission summarized it, the relationship between mafiosi and politicians changed fundamentally in this period of the 50s and 60s.

Support of the Mafia's interests extended beyond the usual electoral and political pay-offs, into newbusiness and speculation deals, but in some cases a new generation of mafiosi assumed positions of power *directly* in the administration of public affairs.

The Mafia controlled everything from cattle rustling and clandestine butchering to provision of water for the city and irrigation of the Conca d'Oro, the city's cemeteries, sale of flowers, contraband in tobacco and drugs, mediation in labour provision for the city's large factories ... and more. Of the 4025 construction licences granted between 1957 and 1963, 80% had been issued to only **five** persons!

A JUDGE INVESTIGATES

In 1979, Giovanni Falcone began working in the Sicilian office of investigating judge Rocco Chinnicici (assassinated 29 July 1983). Judge Falcone's main success was to get testimony from supergrass Buscetta that would lead to the "maxi-trial" of mafiosi in 1987.

When a public building contract was put to tender, the work always went to one company despite other competitive bids – and despite the outrageous price quoted.

If any company (legitimate or not) disputed the informal claim to a construction territory, the mafia clan controlling its tendering company took violent action to end such intrusion.

COMPETITION AND TRADE WARS

Such disputes often mark the beginning of prolonged, acrimonious wars between rival mafia clans, leading eventually to rearrangement of territories – but again only temporarily since peace will last only as long as other challengers are kept violently at bay.

In the early 60s, war broke out between the Greco and La Barbera families over the control of Palermo.

It culminated in the massacre at Cianculli, 30 July 1963, when a bomb in front of the Grecos' house exploded and killed seven of the police squad attempting to defuse it. Mafia violence had begun to turn against the organs of the state itself.

WHAT WAS BEHIND THE ESCALATION IN VIOLENCE?

DID THE MAFIA PERCEIVE A THREAT FROM ITS OWN PROTECTORS?

To understand the Mafia's real dynamic, one has to see that it is not a centralized organization.

Naturally, the Mafia <u>cosche</u> have sometimes formed alliances. One such historic example occured in 1957, in that hotel, when the <u>capi</u>-Mafia decided to expand into drug trafficking.

THE MODERN MAFIA AND DRUGS

In the early 1970s, the Sicilian Mafia moved into drug refining and distribution, particularly heroin. These clans, for whom drug trafficking had been a secondary activity, now began substituting the so-called "French Connection" – Corsican Mafia clans, in fact, operating from Marseilles and Nice who had hitherto dominated the drugs trade.

Profit margins in drugs are very tempting.

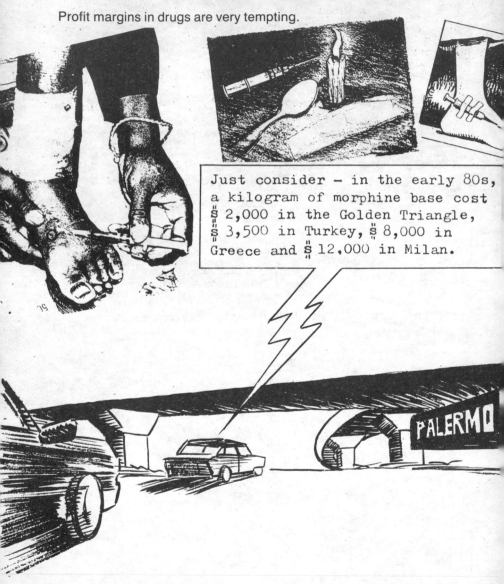

Just consider – in the early 80s, a kilogram of morphine base cost $ 2,000 in the Golden Triangle, $ 3,500 in Turkey, $ 8,000 in Greece and $ 12,000 in Milan.

The profit becomes astronomic if you transform morphine base into heroin -- reaching $ 120,000 per kilogram on the Euro-market and $ 230,000 on the US market!

It is estimated that in the early 80s the Sicilian Mafia supplied one-third of all heroin consumed in the US via New York. Four main secret labs in Palermo refined the heroin. Between 1977 and 1983, the clans realized net profits of $600 million per annum from the sale of heroin to the US alone.

INVESTMENT CAPITAL

First, because Sicily enjoys autonomous status, local banks are not controlled by Italy's central bank in Rome. This means large sums of liquid cash are "available" in local banks.

Second, the State itself transfers huge sums of money for development projects to Sicily every year. More than 30% of this money — thanks to corruption and political inertia — is not spent. Through "clientele connections" with corrupt politicians, the Mafia got access to these funds and invested them in drugs trading.

As the Anti—Mafia Commission revealed, a third source of Mafia money comes straight from the taxpayers' pockets. Four Mafia families control the 334 tax offices in Sicily leased to them by the State. They gain not only from the taxes, but also from various "agents' commissions" (10% as against the Italain national average of 3.3%), and thus have a constant money supply.

MONEY LAUNDERING

ONCE YOU START MAKING BIG PROFITS FROM DRUGS, WHERE DO YOU PUT YOUR ILLEGAL MONEY?

Some of it is of course reinvested in the drugs operation.

Another part is invested domestically in construction, agriculture and the tertiary sectors.

But the largest part is translated into different currencies – Eurodollars, for instance – and enters the international finance circuit. Offshore zones are the most attractive because they guarantee higher secrecy.

Michele Sindona, a financier closely associated with the Mafia, set up a large network of money laundering outlets.

Roberto Calvi, who had dealings with Sindona, created a complete illegal "parallel empire", the Ambrosiano Bank which crashed in 1982. Calvi defrauded the Vatican Bank of $250,000,000.

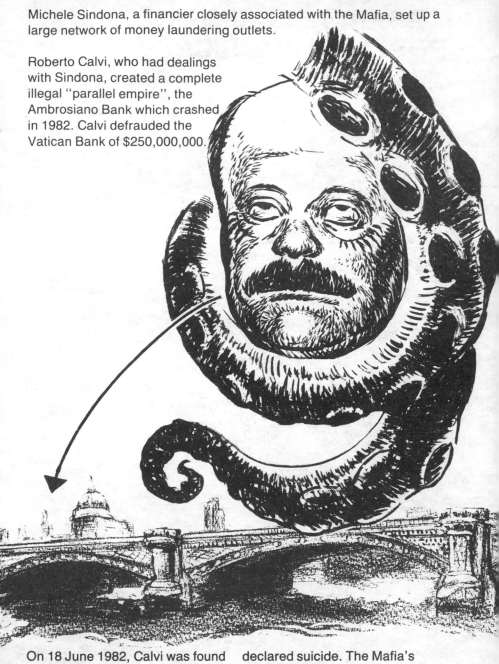

On 18 June 1982, Calvi was found hanged under Blackfriars Bridge in London. His death was officially declared suicide. The Mafia's involvement seems likely, but as usual, unproven.

ORGANISED CRIME IN POST-WAR AMERICA

In 1951, a Senate Committee chaired by the Democrat Senator from Tennessee, Estes Kefauver, uncovered large-scale crime syndicates in America's main cities. More than 20 years after Al Capone's heyday, mobsters were still (and increasingly) active in everything profitable and illegal – gambling, prostitution, drugs, kidnapping and extortion. Like the Sicilians, they laundered their profits through innumerable legal businesses, ranging from horse racing to olive oil importing.

On the spot: Sheriff Walter Clark, of Broward County, Florida, testifies to the Kefauver Crime Committee in Miami, June 1950.

The Senate Committee travelled all over the US. Its hearings, televised to audiences of 20 or 30 million, mercilessly interrogated the "disciples of Al Capone" – mobsters like Frank Costello, Joe Adonis and Albert Anastasia.

Albert Anastasia and lawyer.

Frank Costello

Costello refused to have his face televised.

Joe Adonis

PALERMO

Senator Kefauver's conclusions about the Cosa Nostra's structure remain valid.

A nationwide crime syndicate does exist in the United States of America... This nationwide syndicate is a loosely organized but cohesive coalition of autonomous crime "locals" which work together for mutual profit. (...) So far as we have been able to determine there is no absolute boss of the syndicate, that is, no single person who can give a flat order and have it carried out anywhere in the country.

This is what we have in Sicily too. But the Senator made one important mistake — he saw a more powerful international organization behind the Cosa Nostra, the Sicilian Mafia with a single omnipotent head in Palermo.

Whatever the numerous links between Sicily and America's mafias, the two types of syndicates specialize in different and competing crimes and are entirely autonomous one from the other.

The true extent of Cosa Nostra activities has never been fully assessed, but nowadays its importance has declined and it has had to cooperate with new ethnic syndicates – the Colombian drug cartels, the Chinese Triads and Japanese Yakuza.

Because of the Mafia's complex economic nature, any mapping of its clans, as attempted by some criminologists, will only give a frozen-frame picture representing a moment or short period, but will not reveal a monolithic structure prolonged across time.

Clans have been able to consolidate their power in trust-like "cartels" or "syndicates".

Such cartels have emerged more recently in Sicily, according to my investigations.

A regional 'commission', called **cupola**, hierarchically controls a whole Mafia network, from the provincial **cupola** to individual "families", and down to cohorts of ten (**decine**) individual "men of honour" or "soldiers".

While the apex of Mafia command emerges fairly clearly in the Palermo regional **cupola**, the downward command at local levels has been disputed, and the **cupola** itself has been subject to violent shifts between clans from Corleone and Palermo.

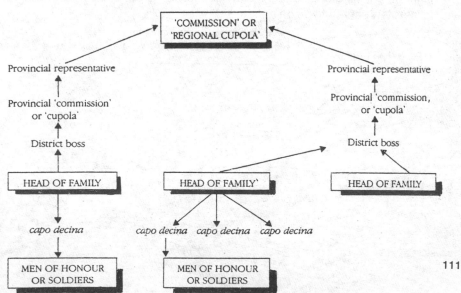

111

First, cutting off one head never paralyses the whole body.

Second, while it's true that some clans have formed cartels, how can we be sure that the captured head represents the apex of the ruling cartel? Might he not instead be a sacrificial head from one of the losing clans, deliberately served to us on a plate?

Falcone's brave and highly competent investigations made him a successful prosecutor of the Mafia – and proved fatal to him. Although he lived under constant high security, the Mafia finally managed to eliminate him on 23 May 1992 in a massive explosion that destroyed his car, killing him and his guards.

Falcone was replaced by an equally courageous judge, Paolo Borsellino, who was also assassinated on 19 July 1992.

113

ILLUSTRIOUS CORPSES

For some time, the Mafia had been waging war on the representatives of the State itself. A series of murders of top officials clearly signalled two things: (1) threats and displays of power to intimidate the Mafia's own high-placed political protectors (**partito**); and (2) direct challenges to the investigating authorities and politicians battling against the Mafia. Here is a list of some Mafia assassinations.

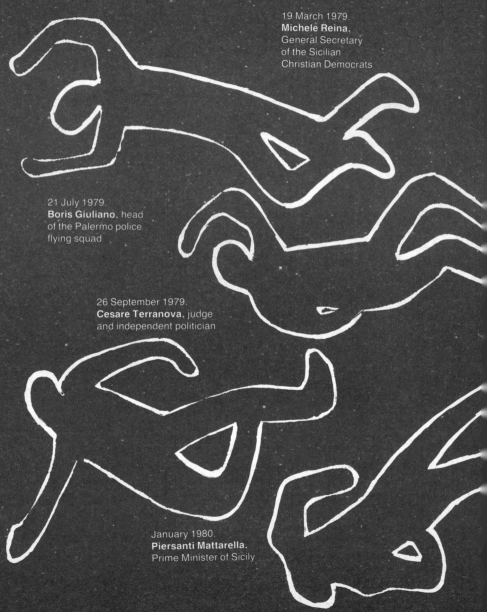

19 March 1979.
Michele Reina,
General Secretary
of the Sicilian
Christian Democrats

21 July 1979.
Boris Giuliano, head
of the Palermo police
flying squad

26 September 1979.
Cesare Terranova, judge
and independent politician

January 1980.
Piersanti Mattarella,
Prime Minister of Sicily

3 May 1980.
Emanuele Basile,
successor to
Boris Giuliano

30 April 1982.
Pio La Torre,
regional secretary of
the Italian Communist Party
(La Torre proposed
the law, introduced
after his death,
which allowed investigation
of bank accounts)

3 September 1982.
General Carlo Alberto dalla Chiesa
(and his wife), Anti-Mafia
High Commissioner and
Police Prefect

and in 1992,
Euro MP **Salvo Lima**
and judges **Giovanni Falcone**
and **Paolo Borsellino**

The Mafia's brazen policy of killings in broad daylight indicated a deeper,
more obscure and sinister game of government collusion, now to be
uncovered.

On 15 January 1993, the **capo** Mafia Salvatore "Totò" Riina was arrested. The press and police hailed this as the beheading of the **capo dei capi**, the head of all heads of the Sicilian Mafia. Riina certainly was a "big fish" – but we should treat with caution the claims of his being the supreme head.

Riina had lived and operated more or less "openly in hiding" for decades. Why suddenly this spectacular arrest? Can he have outlived his usefulness and was now offered as a "sacrificial head" because of some internal change within the Mafia cartels – particularly on the eve of the more spectacular reality – the collapse of Italy's government?

THE END OF COLD WAR CORRUPTION?

When the Cold War ended at the turn of the 1990s, so also did the reason for the Christian Democrats' existence. Its all-pervasive dry-rot corruption had always been known, more or less, but it now became glaringly clear – and intolerable.

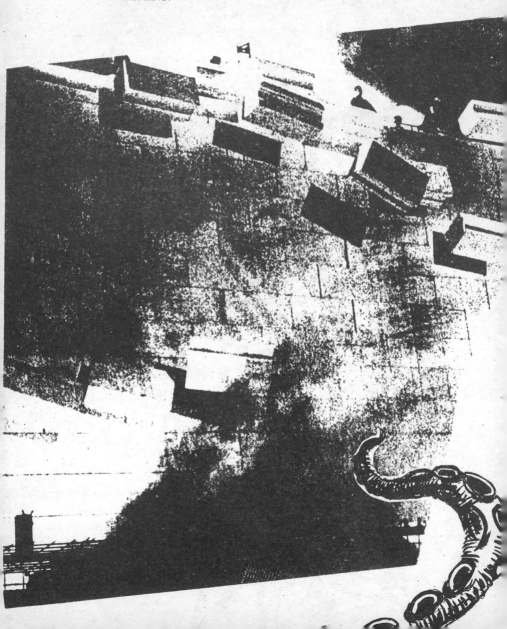

A one-party system had ruled for nearly 40 years by large-scale political and corporate racketeering, with the shady connivance of American and Italian secret agencies, and by a coalition with the Mafia. Christian Democrat and other party politicians corrupted by the system were indicted, the government fell – and the Italian state (a by-product of the Cold War) virtually disintegrated.

A thorough government clean-up – and implicitly a reform of capitalism – would now seem possible. But it is perhaps a little too early to celebrate!

119

THE POSTMODERN MAFIA

Does the arrest of Salvatore Riina mean the Mafia is finished? Let us remember Giovanni Falcone's words – a prophetic forewarning of a new, updated and **global Mafia**.

The current situation, in which criminal organizations from a few countries agree to limited and local pacts is one thing; quite another is the eventual evolution of organized crime towards a federation of vast dimensions. Imagine Turkey's Grey Wolves operating in Germany, allying themselves with Sicilian mafiosi from the United States and Australia, together with the Chinese triads in North America, and all of them moving along the traditional routes of immigration, which are still the surest channels for international crime ... To survive and develop, organized crime needs to rely on local customs and long-established cultures that will protect the secret of their identity from the outside world. At the same time, it needs to create universally valid models on which to base future international liaisons. The extremely dangerous prospect of a homogenized mode of criminal organization, in which a point is reached where one can no longer distinguish between the methods of the Yakusa, the Chinese triads and Cosa Nostra, would create a

kind of global Mafia, and I ask myself how it could possibly be opposed. I can see this global federation taking shape, based on the strong tradition of ethnic groups; on the extraordinary capacity to control territory and to act on decisions; on the development of primitive forms of commerce, such as barter. A Sicilian mafioso could (in fact he already does) trade a kilo of heroin, eighty per cent pure, to a member of one of the Colombian cartels in exchange for three kilos of cocaine: both would profit, because the goods are distributed in different markets. The profit derives from the fact that prices change from country to country, depending on availability.

Fortunately a major obstacle to this grandiose plan already exists: the language barrier. How are people who speak in Sicilian dialect to communicate with others who speak Cantonese or Hong Kong Chinese? Given that, as far as I know, the Esperanto of the underworld does not yet exist, there is still hope...

AH, BUT THERE **IS** A GLOBAL "ESPERANTO"—

IT'S MADE UP OF ENGLISH, COMPUTER COMMUNICATIONS AND DIRTY MONEY.

THE FUTURE
OF AN UNCERTAINTY

Falcone was silenced on the eve of being empowered to investigate the Mafia on a national scale. Rumours sprang up that he was about to uncover a giant financial scandal – and indeed barely a year after his death, the Italian state itself was exposed as a colossal swindle. His assassination was like a replay of Petrosino's murder some 80 years earlier, but progressed at fast-forward to incalculably higher stakes. Falcone died with a prophecy on his lips of a **global mafia**, a nightmare that has already come to short-term fulfilment.

Totally reliable information about the Mafia, from Petrosino's day to Falcone's, was always hard to secure. With the arrival in the mid-90s of "postmodern" multinational mafias, we have entered an era of even greater uncertainty and shakier information. Investigations by law enforcement agencies, even in the US despite all its advanced crime-fighting strategists, are at best fragmentary. We're left with forecasts, speculations and guesstimates.

■ Here is one startling estimate, courtesy of Washington's National Strategy Information Center, circa 1994. The annual worldwide profits of organized crime are put at **$1 trillion**, about the same size as the US Federal budget.

■ Here is a pronouncement typical of the panic inspired by the global threat of organized crime. US Senator John Kerry stated that "organized crime is the new communism, the new monolithic". It is nevertheless agreed that no single worldwide criminal conspiracy exists, no single "board of directors" or head of Crime International.

■ And here's the new way the threat is being met. Intelligence agencies across the globe, from the CIA to Estonia's Security Police, are reorganizing their post-Cold War operations to hunt down gangsters rather than spies.

■ "Mafia" is the term currently applied to any form of syndicated crime anywhere in the world, without specific reference to its Sicilian origins.

Here is a map showing how one European country, Britain, looks threatened in the 1990s by the tentacles of organized crime.

1. California — HELL'S ANGELS

2. Jamaica — YARDIES

3. Colombia — MEDELLIN CARTEL

4. Italy — MAFIA

5. Japan — YAKUZA

6. Russia — CHECHENS

7. Former USSR — VARIOUS

8. Hong Kong — TRIADS

Let's now look at the histories of three so-called "mafias" who are high-stakes players in the global crime game – the Chinese **triads,** Japanese **Yakuza** and the **Colombian** drug cartels. We'll see if a pattern emerges from their activities which gives some clues about the future of the global mafia.

THE TRIADS– A CHINESE MAFIA

The name **triads** refers to the mystical triangular unity of heaven, earth and man. Like the Sicilian Mafia, the triads like to pass off as Robin Hood patriots shrouded in mysterious initiation rites.

The triads began as secret societies opposed to the Manchurian conquerors who founded the Ch'ing dynasty in 1644. Much later, the triads supported Sun Yat-sen's republican revolution which toppled the Ch'ing dynasty in 1911, and they also funded Chiang Kai-shek's war against Mao Tse-tung's Communists.

Demystify the triads and you find a similar cultural pattern akin to the Sicilian and Cosa Nostra mafias – a loose clan structure (fictitious kinship) with a shadowy Dragonhead chief (**capo**), enforcement of secrecy (**omertà**), the respectable fronts of business-cultural associations known as "tongs", and so on.

Like the Cosa Nostra first rooted in immigrant Italian ghettos, the triads have mushroomed from overseas Chinatowns in Amsterdam, New York, London and elsewhere, feeding originally on immigrants through protection, prostitution, gambling, loan-sharking, extortion and drugs.

HONG KONG

The British island colony of Hong Kong became the stronghold of triad societies. Triads in the 1990s began squeezing dry the domestic Hong Kong rackets. They have come under pressure to adapt, because time runs out in 1997.

YEAR ZERO – 1997!

For the triads, 1997 is Year Zero, when Britain hands back its Hong Kong colony to the People's Republic of China.

1. To continue flourishing, the triads must succeed in "going international" and fitting in with a global mafia.

2. China might one day shed its totalitarian Communist regime. The consequences of that are likely to be the same as in Russia – an uncontrolled cowboy capitalism which makes fertile soil for a "mafia" boom.

Triads are already exploiting local corruption in mainland China. But how far they will be able to expand when Communism collapses is unknown.

LET'S EMIGRATE!

In the run up to 1997, the adaptive tactics are clear. Triads have followed the emigrant exodus of Hong Kong business families to North America – especially British Columbia in Canada. Between 1988 and 1993, 115,283 visas to Canada were granted in Hong Kong alone, favouring in particular affluent investors.

Illegal emigration – "people smuggling" – is another triad source of big business. US immigration authorities estimate that between 1991 and 1993, some 80,000 mainland Chinese travelled illegally to Central America en route to the US.

THE TRANSNATIONAL SUPERMARKET

Like kung-fu masters, triads are leaping across national frontiers by adopting the tactics of multinationals, computer communications and an international network of illegal banking.

A typically postmodern scam is **grifting**. Triads equip "grifter tourists" with counterfeit credit cards and send them on a shopping spree all over the world – South Africa, Asia, Western Europe, Canada.

GRIFTING BROUGHT US $200 MILLION WORTH OF FRAUDULENT PURCHASES IN 1991 ALONE!

HIT AND RUN

Triads employ ex-PLA soldiers from the People's Republic of China as gunmen to carry out armed robberies and assassinations in Hong Kong.

The notoriously violent Big Circle Gang (founded by former Red Guards who fled to Hong Kong during the Cultural Revolution) is setting up business in North America.

THE GOLDEN TRIANGLE

Most of the raw opium fo heroin production originates in the Golden Triangle (the northern borderlands of Burma, Thailand and Laos) and (in 1993) is still largely controlled by the warlord Khun Sa.

In the early '80s, Sicilian clans supplied one-third of all heroin consumed in the US via New York. Only 20% of it came into New York from the Golden Triangle. New York narcotics investigators in 1993 claimed the figure topped 80%.

WHERE ARE THE TRIADS GOING?

Triads in 1993 were estimated to have a global membership of 100,000.

Of course, there isn't a single Fu Manchu mastermind with long fingernails running all the triads. Like the Sicilian clans, the triads are loosely organized and often fiercely competitive.

It is not paranoia, however, to fear a global wildfire contagion of triad societies. Triads are gaining more than just toeholds worldwide – in South East Asia, Taiwan, Australia, Japan, Saudi Arabia, Britain, Holland, Canada, the USA and Central America.

Police specialists in narcotics, immigration and fraud have established as fact that links exist between triads, Cosa Nostra and the Yakuza. Falcone's nightmare is, alas, becoming a fact of postmodern life.

ONE EXAMPLE OF TRIADS GANGS INVADING THE USA

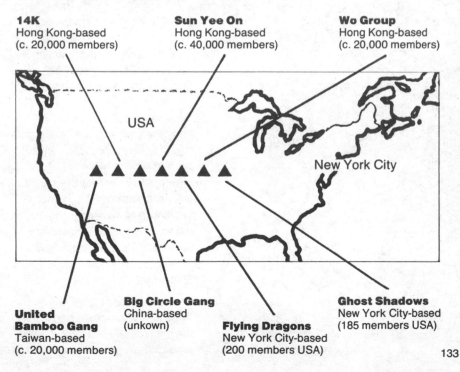

14K
Hong Kong-based
(c. 20,000 members)

Sun Yee On
Hong Kong-based
(c. 40,000 members)

Wo Group
Hong Kong-based
(c. 20,000 members)

USA

New York City

United Bamboo Gang
Taiwan-based
(c. 20,000 members)

Big Circle Gang
China-based
(unkown)

Flying Dragons
New York City-based
(200 members USA)

Ghost Shadows
New York City-based
(185 members USA)

THE YAKUZA'S "ROMANCE"

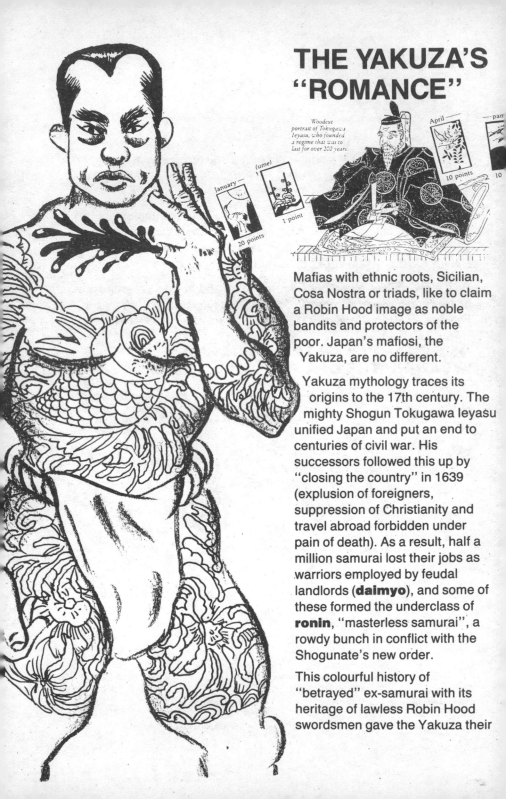

Woodcut portrait of Tokugawa Ieyasu, who founded a regime that was to last for over 200 years.

January

(ume)

20 points

1 point

April

10 points

pam

10

Mafias with ethnic roots, Sicilian, Cosa Nostra or triads, like to claim a Robin Hood image as noble bandits and protectors of the poor. Japan's mafiosi, the Yakuza, are no different.

Yakuza mythology traces its origins to the 17th century. The mighty Shogun Tokugawa Ieyasu unified Japan and put an end to centuries of civil war. His successors followed this up by "closing the country" in 1639 (explusion of foreigners, suppression of Christianity and travel abroad forbidden under pain of death). As a result, half a million samurai lost their jobs as warriors employed by feudal landlords (**daimyo**), and some of these formed the underclass of **ronin**, "masterless samurai", a rowdy bunch in conflict with the Shogunate's new order.

This colourful history of "betrayed" ex-samurai with its heritage of lawless Robin Hood swordsmen gave the Yakuza their

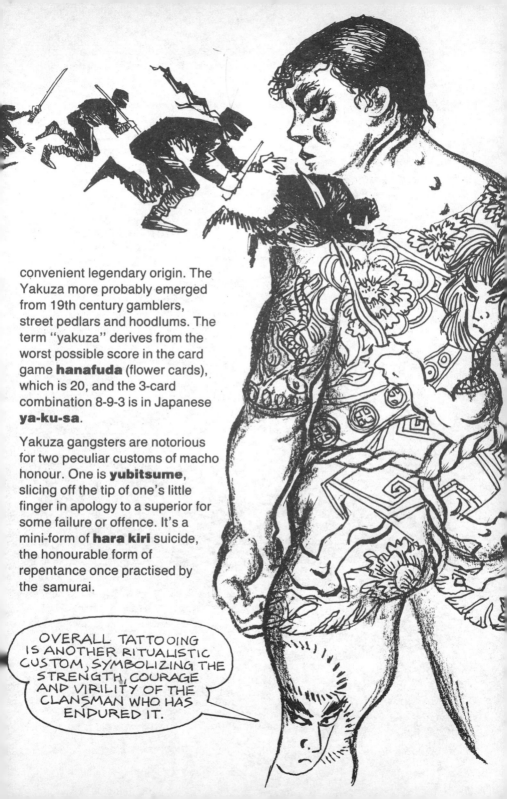

convenient legendary origin. The Yakuza more probably emerged from 19th century gamblers, street pedlars and hoodlums. The term "yakuza" derives from the worst possible score in the card game **hanafuda** (flower cards), which is 20, and the 3-card combination 8-9-3 is in Japanese **ya-ku-sa**.

Yakuza gangsters are notorious for two peculiar customs of macho honour. One is **yubitsume**, slicing off the tip of one's little finger in apology to a superior for some failure or offence. It's a mini-form of **hara kiri** suicide, the honourable form of repentance once practised by the samurai.

OVERALL TATTOOING IS ANOTHER RITUALISTIC CUSTOM, SYMBOLIZING THE STRENGTH, COURAGE AND VIRILITY OF THE CLANSMAN WHO HAS ENDURED IT.

Yakuza clans are structured on the strict hierarchical "boss system" of **oyabun-kabun** (father-child), which mimics the samurai's allegiance to his feudal overlord.

Besides the usual criminal activities, the Yakuza grew powerful through close **ultraright association** with big business and nationalist politics.

One example of this is the ultranationalist association **Dai Nippon Kokusuikai** (Great Japan National Essence Society) founded in 1919 and put to strike-breaking use against the rising trade union and proletarian leftwing movements.

AS BUILDERS, FOREMEN AND LABOUR CONTRACTORS, WE'RE CALLED **KYOKAKU** – "CHIVALROUS PERSONS".

SURE, JUST LIKE US– "MEN OF HONOUR".

UYOKU – THE ULTRARIGHT

Ultraright societies of this type were engaged as private armies by new-rich magnates who profiteered from Japan's economic boom in World War One.

A twilight world connection evolved between the Yakuza underworld and ultranationalists in politics, industry and the military who were agitating for war with Russia and imperial expansion in China, Korea and South East Asia. Secret societies like Dark Ocean (1881) and Amur River (1901), based on Emperor worship and imperialism, gave early warnings of World War Two.

The interesting and unique feature of the Yakuza is its early involvement in **clandestine politics**.

DEFEAT AND OCCUPATION OF JAPAN

The Unconditional Surrender of
Japan in 1945 and its Occupation
under the "Shogunship" of
General Douglas MacArthur,
Supreme Commander of the
Allied Powers (SCAP), looked like
a death blow for ultranationalism
and its underworld accomplices.

The Allies set out with a two-part programme of reform.

1. Root out all ultraright elements in every government department,
finance and industry.

2. Dismantle the giant industrial and financial monopolies (known as
zaibatsu) implicated in the imperial war machine and create a new
democratic free enterprise system.

BUT WHAT
ACTUALLY
HAPPENED?

GYAKU KOSU

What happened was **gyaku kosu** – the "reverse course". Washington policymakers decided that an industrially strengthened conservative Japan would make a useful Pacific ally in the fight against Communism. **The Cold War was declared** – and in the run up to the Korean War (1950), the reform of Japan went into reverse.

a bourgeois revolution always limits itself to democratic transformations which are of advantage to the bourgeoisie itself.

OUCH!

1. The great **zaibatsu** cartels – Nissan, Mitsubishi, Toshiba and others – were not "trust-busted" but refinanced by US big business corporations.

2. The "purge" of ultraright elements in government, the army and big business ceased and went into reverse. G-2 Section of US military intelligence began to recruit ultraright associations to investigate Communist activities.

EXPERTNESS IN THE AREA OF INTELLIGENCE HELPED US TO SAVE OUR SKINS AND **THRIVE** IN THE COLD WAR ERA.

We've already seen how a similar US anti-communist policy in post-war Italy helped to create the Christian Democrats' one-party rule. Much the same happened in Japan. For almost the same number of years, a conservative alliance named the Liberal Democratic Party had one-party control of Japan Incorporated.

Immense, endemic corruption and shady dealings with organized crime were the result in Japan as in Italy.

Gangsters quaintly named "general meetings experts" (**sokaiya**) extorted vast protection sums from terrified shareholders.

Yakuza extortionists were regularly found in industry from the coal face and shop floor to the boardrooms.

In 1960, Prime Minister Kishi Nobusuke called on the ultraright middleman Kodama Yoshio (who'd served a prison sentence for war crimes) to mobilize a paramilitary force of rightwing thugs to supplement the police during President's Eisenhower's state visit.

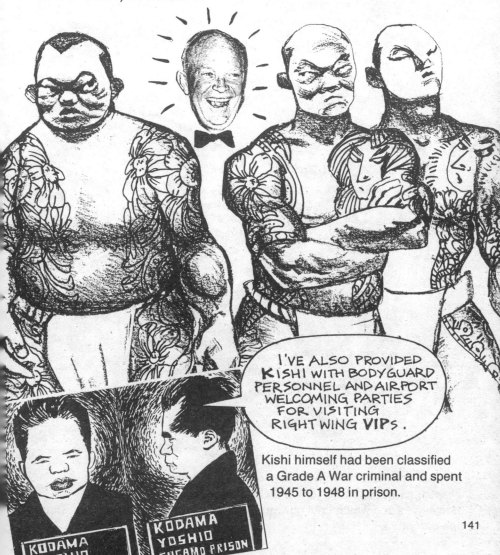

I'VE ALSO PROVIDED KISHI WITH BODYGUARD PERSONNEL AND AIRPORT WELCOMING PARTIES FOR VISITING RIGHTWING VIPs.

KODAMA YOSHIO SUGAMO PRISON

KODAMA YOSHIO SUGAMO PRISON

Kishi himself had been classified a Grade A War criminal and spent 1945 to 1948 in prison.

141

REFORMING JAPAN?

In Japan, as in Italy, a popular wave of post-Cold War discontent seemed to turn against one-party rule and institutionalized corruption. After nearly 40 years, the LDP's stranglehold finally looked broken in the summer elections of 1993 when the New Japan Party swept into power. The NJP leader, Prime Minister Hosokawa Morihiro, promised to uproot corruption and reform the undemocratic system of bureaucracy, the LDP's real power base. Hosokawa's own power base was the urban young consumers – the "baby boomers" – not so traditionally submissive as their parents.

WE'RE FED UP WITH HIGH PRICES.

WE WANT A DEREGULATED FREE MARKET.

WE WANT TO WORK NORMAL HOURS.

Japan's new generation will have to accept the end of the **life employment system** for which their parents willingly sacrificed themselves and which until now guaranteed security, social peace – and one-party rule.

THE RETURN OF THE DINOSAURS

Japan is a country still administered by a class of élite bureaucrats and cliques above government control. In this context, is it really possible to uproot political favouritism and corruption enmeshed with the organized underworld?

Hosowaka's reformist centre-left coalition soon began to fray, resignations followed, and in June 1994 it collapsed. Meanwhile, a Socialist-led minority government has come to power in cynical coalition with the LDP rump. The dinosaurs remain – and that's good news for crime and corruption.

In Italy the news was equally bad for those fighting crime. Silviousconi's media-hyped **Forza Italia** swept into power in dangerous coalition with the neo-Fascist MSI in the South and the right–wing separatist Northern League – an inviting scenario for a Mafia comeback!

COCAINE

The rich world's appetite for cocaine seems bottomless, and profits from it are enormous – but not for the peasants who produce the coca leaves in the Andes (Colombia, Ecuador, Peru and Bolivia).

WE GET BETWEEN $0.5 AND $3.00 PER KILO.

SUBTRACT THE INSECTICIDES, FERTILIZERS, AND WAGES, AND WE'RE LEFT WITH NOTHING – $0.30 TO $0.50 PER KILO.

SO, WHO GETS THE LION'S SHARE?

A 1993 report by the Catholic Institute for Internal Relations (CIIR) tells the story.

In mid-1992 prices in the Huallaga Valley in Peru stood at around $300 a kilo for paste and $900 a kilo for base. Within Latin America it is the traffickers in pure cocaine who earn most. In 1992 cocaine was selling for around $2,000 a kilo wholesale in the Huallaga Valley, $5,000 per kilo in Colombia and around $14,000 a kilo, after export, in the USA. Prices in Europe were even higher. But while Latin American traffickers have amassed breathtaking fortunes, their income still represents a relatively small share of total trade revenue. The two biggest Colombian networks, the Medellín and Cali "cartels", receive between them from 14.2. to 17.1 per cent of the annual retail sales of the cocaine trade, according to the European Parliament's 1991 report. Of this less than 50 per cent is thought to be repatriated to Colombia. The big money is made in the North. In the UK in 1992 "cut" cocaine was selling at between £50 and £60 per gramme, or £50,000 to £60,000 ($72,000 to $86,000) per kilo. Wholesale importers and retailers in the North between them retain from 80 to 90 per cent of the final sales value ...

LET'S TAKE A CLOSER LOOK AT THE MEDELLÍN AND CALI CARTELS.

THE STORY OF A DEATH FORETOLD

Pablo Escobar was a legend, a prototype of the new global gangster who organized an international cocaine distribution network from his hometown base in Medellín, Colombia.

Escobar's fortune was estimated at $3 billion in 1990, laundered in properties and overseas assets which he controlled by fax and computer.

He employed a private army of allegedly 1,000 hitmen in large-scale assassinations of investigators, politicians and policemen, which earned him the title of "narcoterrorist".

Escobar's activities soon began to "overheat", and so he gave himself up to the Colombian authorities and made them a leniency-plea bargain, promising to dismantle his empire. He continued to run his cocaine empire from a custom-built prison in Bogotá.

When in 1992 he escaped and went on the run, a massive manhunt was organized by those who wanted him out of the way – the government's especially assigned police commando unit, aided by CIA tactical advisors, the US Drug Enforcement Administration (even spy satellites and a US C-130 reconnaissance plane were diverted to the hunt). But there were **others** who wanted Escobar dead.

THE CALI CARTEL

A vigilante party was financed by Escobar's rivals, the brothers Gilberto and Miguel Rodriguez Orejuela, who operate a cocaine cartel from their base in Cali. This is a classic example of mafia competition from a more up-to-date efficient organization driving another out of business.

Let's look at some figures.

In 1991, when the Cali bosses stepped up their war against Escobar's Medellín cartel, the Cali syndicate controlled less than a third of the world's cocaine exports. Today it is estimated to control 70% to 85%.

The Cali drug barons are smoother operators, less openly violent, excelling in bribery and PR, and by helping the Colombian authorities to catch Escobar have infiltrated the government and police.

INVESTIGATING FURTHER AFIELD...

Gilberto Rodrigues Orejuela has also approached Colombia's former President César Gaviria with a "surrender" deal similar to Escobar's. The Cali boss wants to go legitimate to protect his colossal assets. The figures speak for themselves. The Organization for Economic Cooperation and Development (OECD) in Paris calculates that about 85 billion's worth of cocaine profits are laundered through the financial markets every year!

Franklin Jurado, Harvard-trained financier, allegedly employed by the Cali cartel, was charged by the Luxembourg police – but, at the time, he was in Russia checking out the new investment frontiers.

The main problem now facing the big cocaine overlords is **too much money** which urgently needs investing. But invested in **what** and **where**?

THE BUSINESS OF LAUNDERING

Laundering comes in many shapes and versions. For instance, an ethnic underground banking network was developed by Indian and Pakistani drug clans, known as **havala** banking. It works very simply.

Suppose a Pakistani heroin dealer in London wants to transfer a big sum of drugs money to the parent company of an international heroin ring. He contacts a havala broker in London . . .

The factory owner who wants the machinery pays his local havala office in Pakistani currency (minus commission). The havala office then pays a local representative of the international heroin ring (minus commission) who will buy more heroin. Everyone is happy.

Chinese triads use a similar form of ethnic chop-shop or stash-house form of banking in North and South America.

ADVANTAGES OF CRIME CAPITALISM

The advantages of international "mafia" banking are obvious – absolute confidentiality and anonymity in the redistribution of vast illegal profits by relatively simple methods.

1. Cash is diversified by front companies and paid into multiple bank accounts.

2. Particularly favoured accounts are off-shore centres (such as the City of London), tax havens (Monaco, Hong Kong, Uruguay) and highly secretive banking centres (Switzerland).

3. Laundering through cash-intensive front businesses – restaurants, supermarkets, real estate and import-export – where accountants can over- or under-invoice accordingly, so that laundered money reappears as originated from legal enterprises.

4. New information technology in the 90s, with its wire services, global computer surfing and satellites, allows cybertech villains to slosh around huge sums of money in virtually untraceable ways.

Let's talk figures again. The estimate for organized crime in Italy alone (combining the Sicilian **Mafia**, Calabrian **'Ndrangheta**, Neapolitan **Camorra** and Apulian **Santa Corona Unita**) puts their liquid funds at about £40 billion in the early 90s.

GO EAST...

After the Berlin Wall came tumbling down, Neapolitan Camorra clans were found inquiring quite openly at Italian consulates for investment possibilities in East Germany.

In its 1993 report, Germany's Federal Police Office highlighted the activities of the Sicilian Mafia in East and West Germany and in former Eastern bloc countries.

Italian restaurants, pizza joints and ice cream parlours make good front venues for laundering drugs money.

Sicilian immigrant communities serve as recruitment bases and hideouts for "hot" mafiosi and gunmen.

SOME ESTIMATES PUT THE COMBINED ITALIAN MAFIA INVESTMENT IN EAST GERMANY AT 70 BILLION GERMAN MARKS, WHICH IS PROBABLY EXAGGERATED.

PRAGUE – A CASE STUDY IN CRIME

Ever since the 60s, Prague was known as a centre of intellectual resistance to Communist tyranny, famous for its dissident writers and intelligentsia. Then, in 1989, came the so-called "velvet revolution" and the Czechs wholeheartedly embraced free enterprise capitalism. Prague suddenly found itself the new frontier town of sleazy cowboy capitalism and organized Eastern European crime.

DRUGS

Prague was chosen as the new crime industry's staging-post because it is ideally situated between Germany and the Balkans route for illegal drugs going west.

Colombians run cocaine from Cali and Bogotá through Sofia in Bulgaria and via Prague to Western Europe.

Prague is also host to a domestic Czech drugs industry – Pervitin, a locally produced amphetamine, and "brown", a cheap poppyseed heroin version.

Prague has its own "boom" of some 10,000 addicts.

RIVAL MAFIAS

Prague has attracted a hoard of "tourist" mafias. Russian gangsters at first monopolized trafficking in drugs, arms, robbery and money laundering.

Krocínova

Karoliny Svétlé

NARODNI

Barto-lomejska

Ostrovni

Vorsilská

They were soon challenged by rival racketeers from all over the east – Poles, Albanians, Serbs, Turks, Romanians, Bulgarians – even some Chinese.

The Neapolitan Camorra seized on Prague as a "nursery school".

WE'RE SENDING OUR "BABY MONSTERS" FOR A LITTLE BASIC TRAINING.

BAH! THEY'RE JUST KIDS PLAYING AT BIG MAFIOSI.

Meanwhile, the grown-up rival gangs are settling their disputes with escalating violence and in the open.

CAR THEFT

Romanians and Bulgarians specialize in stealing luxury Western cars, forging papers for them and sending them on to Poland and Russia.

These crooks are too sophisticated for police methods still designed for small-scale local crime in the Communist past.

WE THINK HALF THE CARS ON PRAGUE'S STREETS ARE STOLEN – BUT WE CAN'T DEAL FAST ENOUGH WILL ALL THIS NEW FREEDOM OF MOVEMENT ACROSS FRONTIERS.

PROSTITUTION

Russians, Serbs and Montenegrins are running prostitution syndicates with Czech girls sent to Italy, Greece and Germany. For the young Lycra-wear entrepreneurs working the Narodni Trida tourist avenue, prostitution looks like easy money.

ARMS DEALING

Czechoslovakia's best-known export and a great favourite with international terrorists was Semtex, the industrial plastic explosive. Ukrainian and other foreign mafias are dealing in stolen Semtex. And there's a good trade in automatic weapons made up of unnumbered spare parts from the former State arms manufacturers.

We picked Prague as the "Dodge City" of postmodern crime, but there are plenty of other East European cities where organized international racketeering has taken root.

GOING TO THE LAUNDRY

The laundering of drugs money is staggeringly big business. Here are a few 1992-1993 estimates: Canada, $10 billion; Britain, $32 billion; Panama, $180 million cleared in US postal money orders through banks . . . and the increasingly unified money markets of the European Union make laundering easier for the new breed of cybertech specialists.

MONEY HAS NO SMELL ATTACHED TO IT.

MAYBE NOT, BUT SOONER OR LATER THESE COUNTRIES ARE GOING TO CRACK DOWN . . .

EVEN THE SAFE HOT MONEY STAS HOUSES, SWITZERLAND AND LUXEMBOURG ARE CLEANING UP THEIR ACT.

THE POST-COMMUNIST MARKETS

Anti-drug crime fighters at Interpol HQ in Paris are trying to weigh up a situation which the Cali and other cocaine kings are already preparing for – the beginnings of a decline in the demand for cocaine in the richer "saturated" markets of Western Europe and America, and, intimately related to this, finding new ways to invest their vast illegal revenues. And these are the reasons why the East European post-Communist world is so attractive, providing new routes and markets for drugs and also new money laundering facilities.

THE LAWLESS FRONTIERS...

Countries of the former Eastern bloc, governed for a long time by Communist regimes, do not yet have specific laws in place against money laundering or other varieties of fraud perpetrated by organized crime, nor do they have updated law enforcement agencies able to deal with "postmodern" racketeers – indeed they are barely able to **recognize** such crimes. A reported $12 billion **disappeared** from the Russian banking system last year...

The fall of State Communism may be viewed as a blessing, freedom for millions in theory, but in fact it is a godsend for the "free enterprise" mafias locally and internationally.

Two things must be understood as crucially affecting the post-Communist economies which make it possible for the parasites of organized crime to thrive.

1. The ongoing, messy transfer of former state enterprises to private entrepreneurs offers a bonanza for the criminal exploitation of **key raw materials**.

Even if cocaine and other drugs were legalized, thus reducing trafficking (a miracle of enlightenment that isn't likely to happen), the mafias will already have established themselves as distributors of petrol, industrial metals and lumber.

FALCONE TALKING TO A LITHUANIAN POLICEMAN

ESTONIA HAS NO COPPER— HOW COME IT'S BECOME THE WORLD'S 6th LARGEST COPPER EXPORTER?

BECAUSE COPPER—AND WHO KNOWS WHAT ELSE?— IS BEING SMUGGLED IN BY RUSSIAN GANGSTERS.

MAFIA GLOBAL TOURISTS

2. The second point is the vanishing of national borders. Before, under strict Communist regimes, personal exit visas were virtually non-existent. Now we live in a global transit space – money is the only visa you really need.

SMART CRIME

Although we live in a late 20th century world of maximum security and supertech surveillance, this seems no deterrent at all to global crime. On the contrary, the new age cybercrooks specialize in types of "smart crime" (complicated financial scams) that high-security techniques are supposed to prevent. The rise of Russian "smart crime" mafias is especially feared.

Some investigators reckon that the Russian mafias **pre**-date the collapse of Communism by 20 years or more – long enough to have outfoxed one system in preparation for taking on another – postmodern capitalism.

Arms dealing is established in Eastern Europe and the market is expanding. But the real nightmare scenario is this – the stockpiles of nuclear weapons, nuclear materials and nuclear technicians with the know-how "for sale" which could fall into the hands of international organized crime. The peril of nuclear arms proliferation is a real menace, not a fantasy!

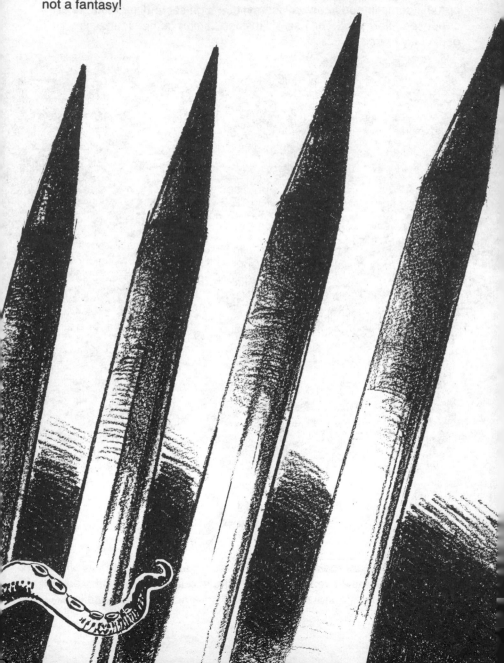

GOOD AND BAD NEWS ON THE GLOBAL MAFIA

There have been some encouraging advances in the fight against organized crime, particularly in Southern Italy and on the Mafia's original home ground, Sicily. Young people in Naples and Palermo have taken to the streets in numerous demonstrations against local mafias. Brave individuals, often women, have defied the traditional code of silence, and their testimony coupled with that of supergrasses has led to successful prosecutions of mafiosi.

Silvio Berlusconi, within the first months of his premiership, brazenly attempted to abolish protective custody for high-ranking officials charged with corruption. His chicanery met with such a mass popular outcry that he had to back down.

There is proof of strategic transnational cooperation between the globally disseminated mafias, but the only good news so far is that no single "mastermind" plan exists coordinating the whole thing.

We have seen how other "mafias", such as Yakuza and triads, resemble the original Mafia model – strong ethnic origins, reliance on local customs of kinship, hierarchy, confidentiality and enforced codes of honour and silence. These features of mafia-style "law and order" do not easily translate from one ethnic group to another, and can therefore limit effective cooperation.

But there is bad news, as we've seen. The worldwide mafias are overcoming their local limits by exploiting the new global information technology.

President Bill Clinton's bright future vision of the **Information Superhighway** ("a network in every American home") overlooks a nightmare scenario. International syndicated crime might well have its own "fast lane" in that Superhighway. Cybertech surfing offers untold possibilities of instant communications and **deceit** for smart crime operators.

Defeat of the global mafia crucially depends on **regulating** and **legalizing** its profitable markets. This is unlikely to occur because of two factors.

1. The weak states of Eastern Europe in the immediate future will provide a reservoir of "bonanza capitalism" for criminal investment and exploitation.

2. So long as the main consumers of cocaine, heroin and other illegal drugs, the US and Western Europe, do not act to legalize and regulate drug consumption through state agencies, the capitalist laws of supply and demand will continue to operate in favour of syndicated crime.

What's the conclusion? The authors of a recent book (1994) on the Colombian cartels, Dario Bétancourt and Marta Garcia, have arrived at the inescapable, naked truth. "Capitalism is the legal mafia and the mafia is illegal capitalism."

FURTHER READING

Titles with asterisks are key books particularly recommended for further reading. UK editions are indicated, but most of these have been published simultaneously in the US.

*Arlacchi, Pino (1983). *Mafia, Peasants and Great Estates: Society in Traditional Calabria*, Cambridge University Press (Italian ed. 1980). Explains why the Mafia developed in some areas, while not in others.

*Arlacchi, Pino (1986). *Mafia Businesses: The Mafia Ethic and the Spirit of Capitalism*, London: Verso (Italian ed. 1983). The best analysis of the modern Mafia by Italy's foremost sociologist on the Mafia.

Balsamo, William & Carpozi, George Jr. (1993). *Crime Incorporated: The Inside Story of the Mafia's First Hundred Years*, London: Virgin Publishing Ltd.

*Blok, Anton (1974). *The Mafia of a Sicilian Village 1860-1960: A Study of Violent Peasant Entrepreneurs*, Oxford: Blackwell. A classic case study by an anthropolgist, also provides a fascinating social history of the Mafia.

*Chin, Ko-lin (1990). *Chinese Subculture and Criminality: Non-traditional Crime Groups in America*, New York: Greenwood Press. Unmystified account of contemporary Chinese Triads in the United States.

*Chubb, Judith (1982). *Patronage, Power, and Poverty in Southern Italy: A Tale of Two Cities*, Cambridge University Press. Excellent analysis of corruption and politics in post-war Naples and Palermo.

Catholic Institute for International Relations (CIIR) (1993). *Coca, Cocaine and the War on Drugs*, London: CIIR.

Dolci, Danilo (1963). *Waste: An Eye-witness Report on Some Aspects of Waste in Western Sicily*, London: Macgibbon & Kee.

*Duggan, Christopher (1989). *Fascism and the Mafia*, New Haven and London: Yale University Press. The most comprehensive account of the Mafia in the fascist period.

Falcone, Giovanni (with Marcelle Padovani) (1992). *Men of Honour: The Truth about the Mafia*, London: Fourth Estate. Judge Falcone, murdered in 1992, talks to French Sicily expert Marcelle Padovani.

*Fentress, J., Wickham, C. (1992). *Social Memory*, Oxford: Blackwell. Excellent chapter 5 on "The Mafia and the Myth of Sicilian National Identity".

Finley, M.I., Mack Smith, D., Duggan, C.J.H. (1986) *A History of Sicily*, London: Chatto & Windus.

Gambetta, Diego (1993). *The Sicilian Mafia: The Business of Private Protection*, Cambridge, Mass.: Harvard University Press.

*Hess, Henner (1973). *Mafia and Mafiosi: The Structure of Power*, Lexington, Mass.: Lexington Books. Classic demystification of mafia as a centralized organization; excellent on mafia structure.

Hess, Henner (1986). "The Traditional Mafia: Organized Crime and Repressive Crime", in: *Organised Crime: A Global Perspective*, ed. R.J. Kelly, Totowa: Rowman & Littlefield.

*Ianni, Francis A.J., Ianni, Elizabeth Reuss (1972). *A Family Business: Kinship and Social Control in Organized Crime*, London: Routledge & Kegan Paul. Excellent 'inside' anthropological analysis of 1960s' American Cosa Nostra families.

Iwai, Hiroaki (1986). "Organized Crime in Japan", in: *Organized Crime: A Global Perspective*, ed. R.J. Kelly, Totowa: Rowman & Littlefield.

*Kaplan, David, Dubro, Alec (1986). *Yakuza: The Explosive Account of Japan's Criminal Underworld*, Reading, Mass.: Addison-Wesley Publishing Company. Comprehensive account of the Japanese Yakusa.

*Kefauver, Estes (1952). *Crime in America*, London: Victor Gollancz. Classic account of the investigations of a US Senate Committee, led by Senator Kefauver, into the activities of 'Al Capone's disciples'.

Mori, Cesare (1933). *The Last Struggle with the Mafia*, London: Putnam. The fascist prefect's own account of his military-style campaign against the Mafia in the 1920s.

*Panteleone, Michele (1966). *The Mafia and Politics*, New York: Coward-McCann (Italian ed. 1962). Classic by veteran Italian anti-Mafia campaigner.

*Raw, Charles (1992). *The Money Changers: How the Vatican Bank Enabled Roberto Calvi to Steal $250 Million for the Heads of the P2 Masonic Lodge*, London: Harvill. Fascinating, if sometimes too detailed, account of the largest financial scandal before the BCCI crash.

*Schneider, Jane, Schneider, Peter (1976). *Culture and Political Economy in Western Sicily*, New York: Academic Press. Thorough Marxist analysis and good social history by two anthropologists.

Sterling, Claire (1990). *The Mafia*, London: Grafton.

Tomasi di Lampedusa, Giuseppe (1961). *The Leopard*, London. Classic historical novel, a sensation in Italy when first published in 1958, describes the decline of an aristocratic family in Sicily at the time of Italian unification in the 1860s. 1961 film by Luchino Visconti.

We have also drawn on current reports and investigations in newspapers and magazines. Readers are urged to keep an eye out for updated features on the global mafias.

The Financial Times (London)
The Guardian (London & Manchester)
The Independent (London)
The Independent on Sunday (London)
The Times (London)

Corriere della Sera (Milan)
Giornale di Sicilia (Palermo)
La Repubblica (Rome)
L'ora (Palermo)

Der Spiegel (Hamburg)
Die Zeit (Hamburg)
Frankfurter Allgemeine Zeitung (Frankfurt)
Süddeutsche Zeitung (Munich)

Newsweek
Time

Acknowledgements

I am grateful for helpful comments on various parts of the text by Dr John Knight and Giuseppe Mastruzzo, as well as Richard Appignanesi's collaborative effort in editing the final text.

Oscar Zarate thanks Judy Groves, Zoran Jetvic, Hazel Hirshorn, Roger Huddle, Giuseppe Muñoz and Marta Rodriguez for artwork and picture research.

Arnd Schneider is an anthropologist specializing in migrations to Sicily and Argentina, and has more recently started to investigate the relationship between contemporary artists and anthropology. He obtained his Ph.D. from the London School of Economics, and has previously published "Emigration und Rückwanderung in einem sizilianischen Dorf" (Return migration to a Sicilian Village, Frankfurt, 1990).

Oscar Zarate, born in Buenos Aires, 1942, was an art director in several advertising agencies there until 1970. He settled in London in 1971 to become a freelance graphic designer and illustrator of comic strips and graphic novels. His works include: *Lenin for Beginners*, *Fatlips* – a children's book with Arnold Wesker, the graphic novels of Shakespeare's *Othello*, Marlowe's *Dr Faustus*, *Geoffrey the Tube Train and the Fat Comedian* with Alexei Sayle, *A Small Killing* with Alan Moore, and he has several works in progress, including *Fly Blues*, a 250 page graphic novel.